INTRODUCING ADAM KADMON

For My Parents
Louis and Evelyn Goldstein

ISBN-13: 978-1542366045
ISBN-10: 1542366046

Alternate Translation Bible (ATB)©
Sheila R. Vitale, Translator

Christ-Centered Kabbalah
Sheila R. Vitale
P O Box 562
Port Jefferson Station, NY 11776-0562 USA
(631) 331-1493

Christ-Centered Kabbalah

Sheila R. Vitale
Pastor, Teacher & Founder
~ The Compleat Kabbalah ~

Ministry Staff
Jesse Aldrich, Elder (McGregor, MN)
Sandra L. Aldrich, Elder (McGregor, MN)
Margaret Mobolaji-Lawal, Elder (Lagos, Nigeria)

Administrative Staff
Susan Panebianco, Office Manager

Technical Staff
Lape Mobolaji-Lawal, Database Administrator
Brooke Paige, MP3 & Software Specialist
June Eble, Shipping Manager

Ministry Illustrators
Cecilia H. Bryant (Oct. 18, 1921 – Oct. 23, 2013)
Fidelis Onwubueke

Music Staff
June Eble, Singer, Lyricist and Clarinetist
Don Gervais, Singer, Lyricist and Guitarist
Rita L. Rora, Singer, Lyricist and Guitarist

The Alternate Translation Bible©

The Alternate Translation Bible (**ATB**) is an original translation of the Scripture.

Alternate Translation of the Old Testament©
Alternate Translation, Exodus, Chapter 32 (Crime of the Calf)©
Alternate Translation, Daniel, Chapter 8©
Alternate Translation, Daniel, Chapter 11©

Alternate Translation of the New Testament©
Alternate Translation, 2 Thessalonians, Chapter 2 (Sophia)©
Alternate Translation, 1st John, Chapter 5©
Alternate Translation, the Book of Jude (The Common
  Salvation)©

Alternate Translation of the Book of the Revelation
  of Jesus Christ to St. John©
Traducción Alternada del Libro de Revelación de Jesucristo©

For Additional Information, please contact:

Christ-Centered Kabbalah
Sheila R. Vitale
PO Box 562
Port Jefferson Station, NY 11776 USA

Christ-Centered Kabbalah
Sheila R. Vitale
Pastor, Teacher, Founder
PO Box 562
Port Jefferson Station, NY 11776 USA

INTRODUCING
ADAM KADMON

Is an Edited Transcript of CCK Message #542.

Introducing Adam Kadmon

Transcribed and Edited For Clarity, Continuity of Thought, And Punctuation by
The *CCK* Transcribing and Editing Team

Formatted as a book by
The CCK Administrative Professional Staff

Introducing
Adam Kadmon

TABLE OF CONTENTS

AN INTRODUCTION TO
THE SEFIROT OF GOD

Kabbalah teaches there is only one living God. The Highest, the Unlimited One, the Infinite One, is inscrutable. There is nothing about Him that we can identify with. He has no attributes. We are incapable of comprehending Him. But there are a variety of attributes or characteristics that we can recognize when He descends low enough for human beings to relate to Him. Therefore, He is descending little by little to reveal himself to the mortal men who are willing to study and reach for Him.

The purpose of deep study is to ascend into the higher planes where God, His mercy, and ultimately eternal life are. God has come down in the form of the Lord Jesus Christ and the gift Jesus Christ bestows upon humanity is called Christ, *Christ in you, the hope of glory.*

Col 1:27

²⁷To whom God would make known what is the riches of the glory of this mystery among the Gentiles; which is ***Christ in you, the hope of glory***:
KJV

We can liken Christ to a spiritual womb. When Christ is grafted, the attributes of God lock onto you and permanently join with you to form an unhindered channel between you (the individual, and, ultimately, this whole plane of existence) and the life giving influences, or the life giving emanations, or the glory (that is the New Testament word) of the world above. Such a union produces eternal life and completely fulfills every human need. There must be a reconnection to the world above. Jesus called it ***the regeneration***.

Matt 19:28

²⁸And Jesus said unto them, Verily I say unto you, That ye which have followed me, ***in the regeneration*** when the Son of man shall sit in the

Humanity has separated from the world above, which is called *the land of the living*, or *the world of the living*, or *the world to come*, and are living in this divided age. We must be rejoined to the world above, which is made available to us in this dispensation through *Jesus Christ*, who is sending this message to Jews, Hindus, Buddhists and Muslims, and eventually the whole world.

Jesus is a spiritual man and His name is a spiritual reality. A name is not a word. A name is the essence of a person, it is their identity, who they are. The teachings of Kabbalah can be reconciled with Jesus, because he is the garment that dresses Primordial Adam in this world, and we are doing it right here in this ministry.

There is a lot of commercial Kabbalah on the Internet today, which is very dangerous. I teach classical Kabbalah, which is for everybody. It is for serious students of the Scripture and people who are sold out to God. Basically, classical Kabbalah gives us the background details of what the New Testament teaches.

People ask me, *Now that you are teaching Kabbalah, do you still believe in Jesus Christ?* Of course I do! Classical Kabbalah calls Ezekiel's Rings, *Sefirot*.

Ez 1:18

> [18]AS FOR THEIR RINGS, THEY WERE SO HIGH THAT THEY WERE DREADFUL; AND *THEIR RINGS* WERE FULL OF EYES ROUND ABOUT THEM FOUR. **KJV**

The ten *Sefirot*, or ten *Rings of Power* of the Kabbalah are appearing to the world today as the Lord Jesus Christ.

There are four spiritual worlds which impact humanity and each of these worlds has ten *Sefirot,* or *Rings of Power. Sefirot* is plural (ends in *ot*). The singular form of *Sefirot* is *Sefirah* (ends in *ah*). All interactions between the spiritual worlds and humanity are through the *Sefirot*.

The right side of Diagram #2 shows *the configuration of Adam Kadmon as a human*. Some *Sefirot* are in the left column and some are in the right column, but ideally we want them lined up in a middle column, because we are looking for balance.

Some of the *Sefirot* are harsh and some are loving. The attributes of God are mixed and blended using a form of spiritual alchemy to become a perfectly balanced expression of the Godhead, for the benefit of humanity.

Humanity is fallen and filled with sin. God would not be God if He did not correct us. It is not acceptable to God for us to have sin in our heart, or to sin against Him, or against our neighbor. He will bless us while we sin as long as we pursue Him, seek to follow after Him, and leave our sin nature behind, to whatever degree we are capable at the moment, because we are ignorant, fallen, spiritual children. He blesses us like we bless our children who make mistakes all the time. But, we cannot continue this way in sin forever. God is blessing us with a form of amnesty while we are growing up.

Some of the attributes of the *Sefirot, Gevurah,* for example, can produce *harsh judgment* in our lives. A demonstration of harsh judgment could be a little boy in a cast from his neck to his feet, the consequence of generational sin. Today, we find the perfect balance of these ten *Sefirot*, or attributes of God, in the form of the Lord Jesus Christ, who has the authority to forgive a family line sin that produced such a harsh judgment.

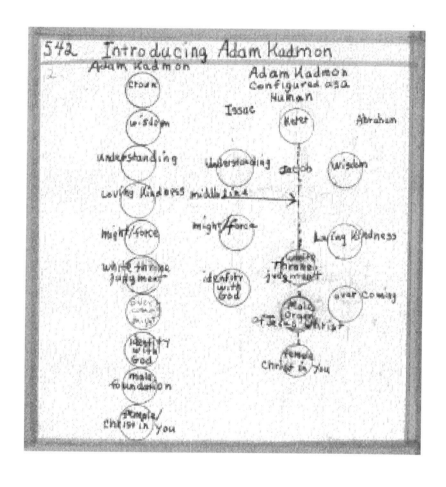

The Quest for Power

The prophets of national Israel sought to ascend in the mind of God. They would meditate on the Hebrew letters representing the *Sefirot*, and blend their various attributes in order to produce the perfect balance, representing the nature and power of the mind of God within themselves. The prophets wanted power over disease and over their enemies. They wanted power in warfare and enough food to eat. We are all looking for power. I want power to overcome the problems of this life and to help you. We need power.

The Danger of Unbalanced Power

There is danger in acquiring the attributes of God in an unbalanced way, because spiritual power, unless it is mixed with loving kindness and judgment of one's own sin nature, produces cruelty. Imbalance of the attributes of God produces a spiritually powerful, cruel man or woman. Cruelty is associated with witchcraft. It is an expression of spiritual power that is not tempered with loving kindness towards your fellow man and judgment concerning your own sin nature.

Balanced Spiritual Power

We are seeking spiritual power which is well balanced, not *equally balanced*, but balanced with loving kindness towards other people, and with an honest judgment of our own contribution to our problems. This balance is called the *middle column*. (See Diagram #2.) When we achieve this balance, we have the hope of manifesting the nature and power of Christ Jesus, the same power that was revealed in Jesus Christ.

Jn 14:12

> [12]VERILY, VERILY, I SAY UNTO YOU, HE THAT BELIEVETH ON ME, *THE WORKS THAT I DO SHALL HE DO*

ALSO; AND GREATER WORKS THAN THESE SHALL HE DO;
BECAUSE I GO UNTO MY FATHER. **KJV**

The Rabbis of national Israel learned how to balance the attributes of God by meditating on the Hebrew letters that represent the individual *Sefirot.* They called down these attributes and balanced them within their mind. They had to find the middle column individually. Today we do not have to meditate like the prophets of National Israel did, because when Jesus Christ said, *I have overcome the world,* He meant that the ten *Sefirot* were completely, permanently balanced within Himself.

Jn 16:33

> [33]THESE THINGS I HAVE SPOKEN UNTO YOU, THAT IN ME YE MIGHT HAVE PEACE. IN THE WORLD YE SHALL HAVE TRIBULATION: BUT BE OF GOOD CHEER; *I HAVE OVERCOME THE WORLD.* **KJV**

Jesus Christ, the glorified man, is the perfect balance of the attributes of God. All we have to do is connect with Him; we do not have to do our own balancing act. *Jesus Christ is the perfect unification of the ten attributes of God.* He is the perfect balance, the middle column **WHICH CANNOT BE UNDONE**.

The Sefirot & The Names Of God

There is a name of God associated with every attribute, or Sefirah. (See Diagram #1.) There is only one God, but He takes different names, just like I am only one person but I am known by different names. My name is **Sheila**, my name is **Mom**, my name is **Grandma**, my name is **Pastor**. I have many names and I am all of these names. In this same manner the Almighty has many names.

The highest **Sefirah** is called **Keter** in Hebrew. It is associated with the word *crown* because it is the highest of all ten attributes. The Keter crowns the other nine attributes and is associated with the name, *I AM*, a translation of the Hebrew word **Ehyeh.** *I AM* is the name of God that was told to Moses when he asked, *Who shall I say sent me?*

<u>Ex 3:13-14</u>

> [13]AND MOSES SAID UNTO GOD, BEHOLD, WHEN I COME UNTO THE CHILDREN OF ISRAEL, AND SHALL SAY UNTO THEM, THE GOD OF YOUR FATHERS HATH SENT ME UNTO YOU; AND THEY SHALL SAY TO ME, *WHAT IS HIS NAME? WHAT SHALL I SAY UNTO THEM?*
>
> [14]*AND GOD SAID UNTO MOSES, I AM THAT I AM: AND HE SAID, THUS SHALT THOU SAY UNTO THE CHILDREN OF ISRAEL, I AM HATH SENT ME UNTO YOU.* **KJV**

The attributes and names of God never appear alone. They always appear in combinations.

The second **Sefirah** is called **Chokhmah** in Hebrew, **wisdom** in English, and is associated with the name of God, **Yah**. The two highest Sefirot, the Keter and Chokmah never descend below because they are too high and exalted. They speak to men through the next lower Sefirah called **Binah**, which means **understanding**.

Binah is the third Sefirah, and is sometimes called **Mother** in the Scripture. Binah is associated with **YHVH** (the **Tetragrammaton**), which Name is translated, **Jehovah**, in the King James Version of the Bible. To fully understand the mysteries of the Scripture, we have to learn the code. **Binah-understanding** can sometimes be called **Mother**, but to reveal the true meaning of any particular Scripture, we have to consider the context of several verses, or the whole verse. Sometimes it is necessary to consider the whole chapter that the word appears in to fully understand what the Scripture is actually saying.

YHVH is the name of **Jehovah** with the vowels removed. **YHVH**, the **Tetragrammaton**, is called **the Holy Name**. Sometimes it is called **the Unique Name**. There is no other name like **Jehovah**. **Jehovah** is the Name that represents God to humanity. He represents the whole Godhead above Him, **Yah** and **I AM**. The **Ein Sof**, which means **the Unlimited One** in Hebrew, is above all the names of God.

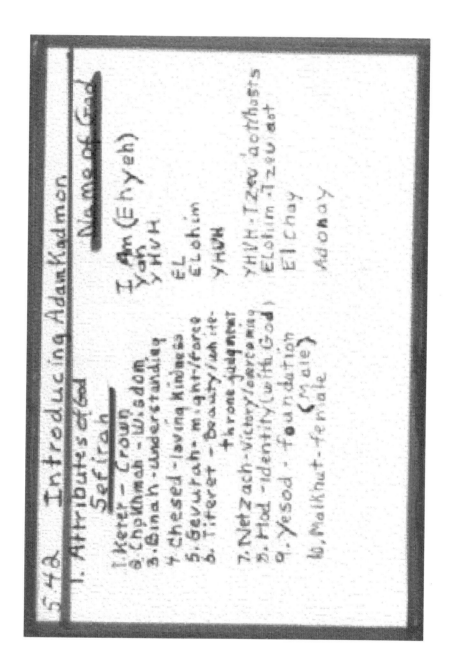

5.4a   Introducing Adam Kadmon

1. Attributes of God

Sefirah — **Name of God**

1. Keter – Crown — I Am (Ehyeh)
2. Chokhmah – Wisdom — Yah / YHVH
3. Binah – understanding
4. Chesed – loving kindness — EL
5. Gevurah – might/force — Elohim
6. Tiferet – Beauty/which it- — YHVH
   throne judgment
7. Netzach – Victory/overcoming — YHVH-Tzev'aot/hosts
8. Hod – identity (with God) — Elohim-Tzev'aot
9. Yesod – Foundation — El Chay
   (Male)
10. Malkhut – female — Adonay

We cannot comprehend *Yah, I Am*, or *the Ein Sof*. We are too fallen. Therefore, *Jehovah* represents the unified, one true God to us. *Jehovah* is the highest level of the Godhead that we can relate to with any degree of understanding, and *Binah* is Jehovah's inner dimension.

A Deeper Understanding

Keter-crown, and *Chokhmah-wisdom*, relate to us through *understanding*, and *Keter-crown* reveals itself to us as *knowledge*. Keter becomes knowledge, wisdom, and understanding. They are inseparable. We are only capable of attaining understanding, and through understanding, we receive wisdom and knowledge.

Why do we take the time to learn complicated spiritual principles like this? Because *eternal life exists in the higher planes*, in the heavenlies. The question is, *How do we ascend?* Many people in the Church are waiting for a physical rapture, but there is no physical rapture. There will be a spiritual ascension, an ascension of mind.

Gen 28:12

¹²AND HE DREAMED, AND BEHOLD *A LADDER SET UP ON THE EARTH, AND THE TOP OF IT REACHED TO HEAVEN: AND BEHOLD THE ANGELS OF GOD ASCENDING AND DESCENDING ON IT.* **KJV**

We climb Jacob's ladder by thinking about the same things that the Lord thinks about. Everything in our lives depends upon what our mind focuses on. Physically, we are the material food that we eat, and spiritually, we are the spiritual food that we eat. *We are what we think*.

If we focus on the high doctrine of God, we will ascend in the Spirit. If we continue to pursue difficult deep teachings (by submitting ourselves to God, who will help us understand them), we will begin to ascend and ultimately arrive at the level of consciousness where there is no death. We climb Jacob's ladder with our mind, or our thoughts.

The fourth Sefirah is called ***Chesed*** in Hebrew, which means ***loving kindness***. ***Chesed*** is associated with the name of God, ***El***. God takes on a particular name when he performs or behaves in a certain manner, which describes that behavior. Once you learn the qualities of the ten Sefirah, you will be able to identify the Names of God and the Names of the corresponding Sefirot, as you read the Scripture.

There are deep, exciting mysteries of the life and the truth of God underneath the surface of the King James translation, which is on a parable level. Studying the principles of the Sefirot gives us a deeper understanding of the written Word, and the ability to unlock these difficult Scriptural principles. A pursuit of the knowledge of the Scripture places us on the track to ascend to the Keter, the highest place where Jesus exists. In Kabbalah, it is taught that it is impossible to attain to the level of ***Keter***. One can only attain to ***understanding***. In Christ Jesus, though, we have the whole ball-of-wax. ***Christ in you, the hope of glory is the New Covenant.*** Jesus Christ is the New Covenant, but the Church today is not living in the New Covenant.

Col 1:27

> ²⁷TO WHOM GOD WOULD MAKE KNOWN WHAT IS THE RICHES OF THE GLORY OF THIS MYSTERY AMONG THE GENTILES; WHICH IS ***CHRIST IN YOU, THE HOPE OF GLORY***:
> KJV

When you live out of Christ you experience the New Covenant, but He has to graft to you, mature in you, and you have to die to the lifestyle of the Fiery Serpent, which is your carnal life. If you are still thinking with your carnal mind and living a carnal lifestyle, you are not living out of Christ.

The man, Jesus of Nazareth, who was born of a woman, completely emptied Himself of everything, and every desire which had to do with this world. He was so completely filled with the life of Christ, that after His body was killed, His spirit and soul ascended to the Father. You can experience both worlds for a season, but ultimately ***you cannot have eternal life and the life of this world***.

Spiritual Alchemy

The fifth Sefirah is called *Gevurah* in Hebrew, which is associated with *might or force*, and the name of God, *Elohim*. *Gevurah* is tempered by *Chesed-loving kindness*, which is across from it. *Tiferet-beauty*, the sixth Sefirah, which is right below Gevurah, when blended with Gevurah and Chesed becomes either a *force of destruction,* or *justice*.

These three Sefirot, the fourth, fifth, and sixth, *Chesed-loving kindness*, *Gevurah-might or force*, and *Tiferet-beauty*, together are called *the White Throne Judgment*. (I did not receive this revelation from Kabbalah, but through a word of knowledge, that *Tiferet-beauty* represents the White Throne Judgment.)

Gevurah, blended with loving kindness towards other people, blended with the White Throne Judgment of introspection, or judgment of your own sin nature, makes you a powerful, spiritual person in Christ Jesus.

I talked earlier in this message about *spiritual alchemy*, which is the mixing of the different attributes of God to attain to a balance When we mix *Gevurah-might,* or *force,* with *Tiferet-beauty (the White Throne Judgment)* and *Chesed-loving kindness*, the result is the miracle working power of the nature of God.

The seventh Sefirah is called *Netzach-overcoming power,* or *Victory*, which is the power to endure in the face of difficulties and hardship. It is the attribute of God which overcomes all things. Jesus said, *If you overcome all things, you will enter into the world above.*

Rev 21:7

> ⁷HE THAT *OVERCOMETH SHALL INHERIT ALL THINGS*; AND I WILL BE HIS GOD, AND HE SHALL BE MY SON.
> KJV

The eighth Sefirah is *Hod*, which means *identity*. *Hod* is the ability in Christ Jesus to recognize Christ both in ourselves and in other men, because the world cannot recognize Christ.

Paul said, ***The world cannot discern us***, which means, they cannot figure out who we are, so they feel threatened and sometimes try to kill us. He said, ***Only we can discern each other***, meaning, ***Only Christ can discern Christ.***

1 Cor 2:15

> [15]BUT HE THAT IS SPIRITUAL JUDGETH ALL THINGS, YET HE HIMSELF IS JUDGED OF NO MAN. **KJV**

2 Cor 5:16

> [16]WHEREFORE HENCEFORTH KNOW WE NO MAN AFTER THE FLESH: YEA, THOUGH WE HAVE KNOWN CHRIST AFTER THE FLESH, YET NOW HENCEFORTH KNOW WE HIM NO MORE. **KJV**

Yesod, called ***foundation***, is the ninth Sefirah. ***Yesod*** is the ***male***. All of the previous eight attributes of God flow down into Yesod, which acts as a funnel. Yesod is the foundation which collects all of the power, or the emanations, of the eight attributes above it.

All of the attributes of God, from the first through the ninth Sefirot, are in the world above, but ***Malkhut***, the tenth, is ***Christ in you***. There is a division between Yesod, the ninth, and Malchut, the tenth Sefirah. These nine Sefirot above, want to marry Malkhut, Christ in you. It is the same message I have been preaching for years, the same message as the surface Scripture, ***there is going to be a marriage***.

Rev 21:2

> [2]AND I JOHN SAW THE HOLY CITY, NEW JERUSALEM, COMING DOWN FROM GOD OUT OF HEAVEN, PREPARED AS A BRIDE ADORNED FOR HER HUSBAND. **KJV**

Rev 19:9

> [9]AND HE SAITH UNTO ME, WRITE, BLESSED ARE THEY WHICH ARE CALLED UNTO THE MARRIAGE SUPPER OF THE LAMB. AND HE SAITH UNTO ME, THESE ARE THE TRUE SAYINGS OF GOD. **KJV**

Christ in us (Malkhut) is going to marry the glorified Jesus Christ, and the glorified Jesus Christ contains all of the nine Sefirot (attributes) of God. The glorified Jesus Christ has the ability to mix and match these attributes to form different spiritual solutions, or different grades of spiritual power, to perform miracles and meet different needs.

When Christ is grafted to us here in the earth, we are *female*. When Christ in us (the lowest Sefirah, the female, which is *Malkhut*), marries the **manhood** of the Sefirot (the Lord Jesus Christ who contains all nine Sefirot), our connection to the world above becomes permanent, and we receive everything from the *Keter* on down, right here in the flesh. In addition, we receive life, and our physical bodies become the *land of the living*. Jesus said, *I am the way, I am the truth, and I am the life. Marriage to Me gives you eternal life.*

Jn 14:6

> ⁶JESUS SAITH UNTO HIM, *I AM THE WAY, THE TRUTH, AND THE LIFE*: NO MAN COMETH UNTO THE FATHER, BUT BY ME. **KJV**

People say, *Jesus Christ is the hope of glory. He is eternal life. I am saved!* But, how are you saved? I just explained to you how He is saving us by applying the principles of Kabbalah. It is the same message. There is no difference between the spirit of the Old Testament and the New Testament. There is only a difference in the translation, and in the understanding. Anyone who grasps the spirit of the Scripture knows that the New Testament is the same as the Old Testament.

Today, the Jews who have been converted are basically secular, non-practicing Jews. It is hard to convert a Jew who has been educated in the Scripture and Kabbalah with the message being preached in the Church today because those Jews know that any new revelation coming down must line up with, and cannot contradict the existing Scripture.

It is so hard to convert a learned Jew, because the doctrine in the Church today is largely in error. It is true Jesus Christ is the Son of God, but we must explain who Jesus Christ is to the Jew using Kabbalah, like I just explained it to you. You cannot expect people who have been studying the Scriptures for generations to take your word for it when you tell them, *Jesus Christ is the Son of God*. They are entitled to an explanation, which the Church today is not capable of delivering.

Partnership

The Names of God which minister the White Throne Judgment are *Jehovah Adonai*, a combination, or a partnership of Jehovah and Adonai. *Adonai* is the name of God associated with the tenth Sefirah, *Malkhut*, Christ in you. If you have Christ in you, that means *Adonai* is the Spirit of Christ operating in you. We are concerned with spiritual principles; the way we explain it does not have to be an exact match.

For the purpose of this message, let us say Adonai is the Spirit of Christ. The White Throne Judgment is the judgment of your own sin nature. Adonai, the Spirit of Christ, cooperates with the God World above, which we are connected to through the glorified Jesus Christ, to destroy your sin nature. It is a partnership, or a collaboration. Kabbalah says the Name of God associated with *Tiferet-beauty* is the Name *Jehovah Adonai*, heaven and earth working together to make a particular vessel worthy for Jesus Christ to express Himself through. You are worthy when your sin nature is under the feet of Christ Jesus. The White Throne Judgment (*Tiferet-beauty*) is the repression, judgment, and punishment of your ugly side, which is your sin nature, and this judgment makes you beautiful.

The Name of God associated with *Netzach-overcoming* is *Jehovah Tzevaot*, which means *the God of hosts*. The Name of God associated with *Hod*, the ability to *identify* the mind of Christ is *Elohim of hosts*.

El-Chay is the Name of God associated with *Yesod*. *Chay* means life. Life is associated with *Yesod*, the *male,* because when *Yesod* joins in an act of spiritual sexual union with *Malkhut*, which is Christ in you, he gives life to Malchut, the female.

Jesus came to give life to this dead world. It is not a dying world, it is a dead world, and the way He gives us life is by

14

joining His lower parts to Christ in us. It is a spiritual sexual union, or marriage. The definition of true marriage is sexual union. You are not married because you have a ceremony or say, *I do*. You are not married because you wear a ring. For generations societies did not consider you truly married until the *physical consummation.* We are engaged to Jesus Christ but not married to Him. We will not be married to Him until the union is fully accomplished, and the proof of the union is the birth of His Son. You and I shall be saved in childbearing when we bear the man child of Revelation, Chapter 12, which will save us from our own sin nature.

1 Tim 2:15

¹⁵NOTWITHSTANDING SHE SHALL BE *saved in childbearing*, IF THEY CONTINUE in FAITH AND CHARITY AND HOLINESS WITH SOBRIETY. **KJV**

The Fullness of Christ

Christ is grafted to us in seed form, and the seed has to mature into Christ Jesu, by warring with Satan. In order for a seed to sprout, it needs water, and Satan is the spiritual water. Every man has a measure of spiritual energy, or spiritual water. Christ, the grafted seed, wars with Satan, and the ultimate warfare is that He boils her. The parable of the spiritual warfare between the grafted Christ and Satan in the individual, is that Satan will be boiled.

Christ wars against Satan, who is represented by water. The warfare creates heat, which boils and distils her. The impurities remain in the ground, and Christ captures the condensate, the vapor which ascends as a result of the distillation. The seed sprouts and Christ grows up into Christ Jesus, who is capable of marrying the glorified Jesus Christ. Christ in us is the hope of our glorification, but it is a fight, a warfare, a whole process. We do our part through this kind of deep study, spiritual warfare, and warring against our own sin nature.

Then there is the male child, the offspring of the glorified Jesus Christ, who will save us.

Rev 12:5

5 AND SHE BROUGHT FORTH A MAN CHILD, WHO WAS TO RULE ALL NATIONS WITH A ROD OF IRON: AND HER CHILD WAS CAUGHT UP UNTO GOD, AND TO HIS THRONE. KJV

The glorified Jesus Christ comes down and joins permanently with the spiritual child in us. I heard somebody saying, *He already came.* Yes, He came as the Holy Spirit. The Holy Spirit is just His arm. ***The whole man is coming***, and He will save us through a permanent union with himself. But, in order for Him to join with us permanently, there must be something inside of us for Him to join with, which is Christ in you, your hope of glorification.

Jesus Christ can enter into this world in absolute fullness, but, if you do not have Christ, if there is nothing in you to hold onto His emanations (His glory, His Spirit), He will come and He will go, and you will be the same as you were. The Holy Spirit is likened to water: It falls on you and then drains off of you. After that, whatever is left dries up, or evaporates.

Christ is signified by oil; He sticks to you. When the glorified Jesus Christ comes down, He will cleave to the oil, which is his son in you. There will be a permanent union between the glorified Jesus Christ and Christ Jesus in you, and that is the fullness of God. That is the double portion the glorified Jesus from above (from heaven) and Christ Jesus in our earth. The marriage is a permanent union, which fills us with His life.

In order to be prepared for the joining, we need an organ, Christ Jesus, present in us to receive Him. The preparation involves the exposure of the sin nature, the rejection of it, the warring against it, and of course, a knowledge of the Scripture. We ascend in knowledge, which comes from deep study. We are going up a staircase, known in the Scripture as ***Jacob's ladder***. It is a process.

What does *fear and trembling* mean? Fear means respect of God, because when you respect Him, He respects you. When you turn towards Him, He turns towards you. God is no respecter of persons, but it is hard to get the blessings from the Lord when your back is to Him. You cannot receive His blessings when you are walking away from Him, or rejecting Him, or insulting Him,.He does not withhold anything from anyone. Our attitude, which comes out of our sin nature, separates us from Him. Satan does not want us to have the blessings of God.

Adam Kadmon

Adam Kadmon is the foundational principle of Kabbalah. *Kadmon* means *primordial*, and *Adam Kadmon* means *Adam*, who is the *primordial,* or the *first human*. In Diagram #2, Adam Kadmon is configured, or described to us, in two different ways: 1) As a descending line of the attributes of God as he descends into the lower planes, and 2) Configured as a human, as described in the three columns of the Sefirot, the attributes of God.

Adam Kadmon appeared on a very high plane of consciousness. He is closest to the Unlimited One (Ein Sof). He is a channel, a vehicle, for the light and the life of the Ein Sof to filter through. If the unhindered life of the Unlimited One were to pour into us, it would destroy us. Jesus clearly stated this principle, saying, *If you put new wine in an old wine skin, the wine skin will be destroyed, and the wine will pour out*.

Matt 9:17

[17]NEITHER DO MEN PUT NEW WINE INTO OLD BOTTLES: ELSE THE BOTTLES BREAK, *AND THE WINE RUNNETH OUT, AND THE BOTTLES PERISH*: BUT THEY PUT NEW WINE INTO NEW BOTTLES, AND BOTH ARE PRESERVED. **KJV**

Adam Kadmon is the primordial being. We do not know what He looks like, but he is not humanoid. The light and Spirit of the Infinite One poured into and filtered through Him in measured amounts, which were used to form four worlds: *The World of Emanation, the World of Creation, the World of Formation, and the World of Action*. The whole world as we know it, is *Adam Kadmon, because* each of the four worlds, which slowly descended, are within Him. We are in the lowest world, which is called the *World of Action*.

Adam Kadmon is the beginning of the creation of God. He is the primordial human, the creation of God at the beginning of time. In the Book of Revelation, the Scripture says that the glorified Jesus is the beginning of the creation of God.

Rev 3:14

[14]AND UNTO THE ANGEL OF THE CHURCH OF THE LAODICEANS WRITE; THESE THINGS SAITH THE AMEN, THE FAITHFUL AND TRUE WITNESS, *THE BEGINNING OF THE CREATION OF GOD*; **KJV**

Rev 22:13

[13]I AM ALPHA AND OMEGA, *THE BEGINNING AND THE END, THE FIRST AND THE LAST.* **KJV**

When Jesus said, I am the first and the last, He meant, The Inscrutable One has come down to the earth to dwell with us. He also said, I am the beginning and the end. He meant, I am the personality that reveals Keter, **the unknowable Sefirah**, and I am also the personality that reveals **Malkhut**, the knowable Sefirah. It is the same principle.

Jesus is the personality that revealed Adam Kadmon at the beginning, and He is also the personality that reveals Adam Kadmon in the earth today. Adam Kadmon never left the highest planes of consciousness, He just put down aspects of Himself, like a plant puts out shoots or feelers. It would be like putting your arm down into a hole in the ground but your body is up here above the earth.

Jesus said, **I am the beginning and the end, I am the first and the last**, meaning, **I reveal Keter the crown, and I also** reveal Malkhut in the earth, or **I reveal Primordial Adam above, and I also reveal Primordial Adam appearing in a human being**.

Configured As a Human

The great teachers of Kabbalah configured Adam Kadmon as a human to be a teaching tool, to help students of Kabbalah understand his spiritual principle. The ten attributes (Sefirot) of God are arranged in three columns. There are three Sefirot on each side, and three in the middle. I said earlier in this message there needs to be a perfect balance of the attributes between the left side (strength) and the right side (kindness).

Left Side & Right Side

The strength of God: *Binah*-understanding, *Gevurah*-might and force, and *Hod*-identity with Christ, are on the left side of the configuration.

Binah, who can be likened to a female lioness, is understanding. She also represents judgment. We are expected to clean up our act in accordance with the understanding we receive as soon as we receive it,. For example, if you are in fornication and you listen to a message which says that God does not accept fornication in people who are following Him, you are expected to come out of fornication. If you do not come out of fornication, then you are in danger of contracting a disease or some other judgment.

Binah's warning is kind, merciful judgment, which says, *Get out before you have to suffer a consequence!* If you do not heed the warning, *harsh judgment* will eventually fall on you. *Understanding* comes with judgment because you cannot understand the things of God unless your carnal mind is judged. We are all unable to understand because Satan blocks up our ears. The Scripture clearly indicates that Satan is the one who produces deafness, and that her judgment is *silence*.

The operation of Satanic activity produces deafness. You do not have to be a black witch for this to happen. Satan has both an evil side and a good side, which operates on the social plane. She is involved in envy, backbiting, gossip and hatred. No matter how you try to cover up your ungodly behavior and tell yourself that you are talking about someone for their own good, it is actually Satan, operating of on a social level, in the life of a *good person*.

Our deafness must be dealt with if we are to receive understanding. A very small percentage of the population is capable of understanding Kabbalah (which *is* the Doctrine of Christ, because they are the same message, coming from two different vantage points), but most people do not understand why they cannot understand. Jesus asked the Pharisees, ***Why do you u not understand my speech?***

Jn 8:43-45

[43]*WHY DO YE NOT UNDERSTAND MY SPEECH? EVEN BECAUSE YE CANNOT HEAR MY WORD.*

[44]*YE ARE OF YOUR FATHER THE DEVIL*, AND THE LUSTS OF YOUR FATHER YE WILL DO. HE WAS A MURDERER FROM THE BEGINNING, AND ABODE NOT IN THE TRUTH, BECAUSE THERE IS NO TRUTH IN HIM. WHEN HE SPEAKETH A LIE, HE SPEAKETH OF HIS OWN: FOR HE IS A LIAR, AND THE FATHER OF IT.

[45]AND BECAUSE I TELL YOU THE TRUTH, YE BELIEVE ME NOT. **KJV**

The Pharisees did not understand because Satan, the unconscious part of their carnal mind, blocked it. Satan represents sin in your life, so understanding comes with built-in judgment, to bomb Satan out of the way.

If you cannot understand, it is because your heart (motive) is not pure, but the Lord does not condemn you, He brings judgment which will clear away the impurity so that you can understand. If you are seeking the understanding of God, prepare to face your sin nature, because understanding comes with judgment. Once you make a commitment to the Lord, He will not end the judgment when you start screaming, ***Lord, get me out of here!***

Gevurah-might or ***force*** is also on the left side of the configuration. It is associated with the name of God, ***Elohim***. If this attribute is not tempered by loving kindness, or one of the positive Sefirot on the right side, it can be destructive, because there is judgment for sin.

There is judgment of God for sin *with mercy*, and there is judgment *without mercy*. God deals with us in all different ways, depending on how troublesome our carnal mind is. He does not want to rain down judgment on us, but if He intends to save our life and your carnal mind is in the way, judgment must fall. That is the bottom line. He prefers mercy and truth. He will tell you: *This sin is in your heart*. Then, when you try to stop doing it in your own power, but cannot, the paddle is necessary. Hopefully the Lord will bring judgment with mercy and not *Gevurah*, the harsh judgment of the Lord, alone.

The last Sefirah on the left side is *Hod*, which is the *ability to identify Christ*. Adam Kadmon's left side signifies judgment on two levels: 1) Understanding, which is *judgment with kindness* through Christ, or 2) Judgment *without kindness,* through Satan, the Enforcer of Jehovah's Righteous Sowing & Reaping Judgment.

The three Sefirot on Adam Kadmon's right side are *Chokmah-wisdom, Chesed-loving kindness*, and *Netzach-power to overcome*. We need power to overcome our carnal mind, and that power is formed through a spiritual alchemy, a blending of the overcoming power of the Sefirot on the right side, and Binah and the might and force of Gevurah on the left side.

Ascension through The Middle Column

You cannot overcome Satan without power. All of the Sefirot are mixing and matching with each other and the perfect balance is called the *middle line,* or *the middle column*. When the four attributes in the middle column are lined up and communicating with one another (because it is possible for them to have their backs to each other), it means that their *glory, emanation, spirit*, or their *qualities* are blending into one power. A person in this configuration will be in perfect order.

In other words, if Christ Jesus, which is *Malkhut*, the female (Christ in me) is connected with the glorified Jesus Christ up in the crown center (**Keter**) I am in perfect order, and the glory of eternal life is pouring into me, down here in the flesh. This is spoken about in Revelation, Chapter 12.

Rev 12:1

> ¹AND THERE APPEARED A GREAT WONDER IN HEAVEN; A WOMAN CLOTHED WITH THE SUN, AND *THE MOON UNDER HER FEET, AND UPON HER HEAD A CROWN OF TWELVE STARS*: **KJV**

In this Scripture, the woman is in perfect order: The moon is under her feet and the stars are over her head. She is in perfect order to receive the salvation of God.

Kabbalah relates the three columns of the Sefirot of Adam Kadmon to the three biblical patriarchs: Abraham, Isaac and Jacob. Each of these biblical characters embodies the qualities of one of the three column.

The **middle line** of Adam Kadmon is called **Jacob**, representing compassion (**Tiferet)**, a balance of the left and the right side. The **left side** is identified with **Isaac**, which is **harsh judgment**, a man with strong spiritual power used for the wrong motives. The **right side** signifies **Abraham** and represents kindness and goodness. But we are looking for is a blend of them all. You cannot have a perfect middle line which ascends into eternal life without judgment. We are down here in the tenth Sefirah, which is **Malkhut,** the female, Christ in you, the hope of glory.

Yesod is the glorified Jesus Christ, the **male organ** of Christ Jesus. Christ Jesus ministers the **White Throne Judgment**, and His male organ descends from **Yesod** to join with Malchut in the individual, in an act of spiritual sexual intercourse.

All the Sefirot of God are depicted as circles or spheres because they are three dimensional like the planets. They spin on their axes, and they also rotate in an orbit. The four Sefirot in the middle column need to be facing each other to blend their attributes.

The **White Throne Judgment (Tiferet) signifies Christ Jesus**, and **Keter signifies the Lord Jesus Christ**. These two

Sefirot blend their attributes, and that power is funneled down into *Yesod,* the spiritual male organ of Christ Jesus, which delivers the power, or energy, to Malchut in the individual. Christ Jesus is also capable of grafting Christ to individuals who do not have Christ. Everything depends on your dealings with your own sin nature. You ascend when everything is lined up in the right order. If you are not looking at your sin nature, your back is to Christ Jesus.

This is the teaching of Kabbalah in a nutshell: ***The powers of the world above are coming down to dwell in us and that is how we experience spiritual ascension.*** It is also expressed that way in the Scripture, that our ascension is spiritual, and the reality is that ***the powers of the world above come down to dwell in us***.

Gen 28:12

> [12]AND HE DREAMED, AND BEHOLD A LADDER SET UP ON THE EARTH, AND THE TOP OF IT REACHED TO HEAVEN: AND BEHOLD THE ANGELS OF GOD **ASCENDING** AND DESCENDING ON IT. **KJV**

Ascension means that we experience the world above, but we do not leave the earth. We are in heaven and earth at the same time. Jesus had this experience. He was in a physical body, but all of the highest powers from above were dwelling in Him right down here on earth.

He had all the wisdom, knowledge, understanding, loving kindness, overcoming power, and power of God right down here, in the flesh. That is the promise of salvation. It is not leaving the earth, it is not living in a mansion, it is not walking on physical streets of gold.

Salvation Means Safety

Salvation is possessing the earth of our physical bodies, and having all of our needs met. Salvation means safety; possessing the earth in safety.

We are not safe in this world. People who think they are safe are spiritually naive. We could be in a car accident tomorrow, and die. We could walk out of this room and have a brain aneurism. We are not safe. We do not know what is coming tomorrow, or the next minute, or the next second.

Most people, at least in this country, are so privileged that they walk around in a state of total denial about what might happen to them. They do not want to walk in fear and have no power over these things, so they deny the reality that our lives are in danger every second of every minute, of every hour, of every day. The Lord wants us to know about the dangers of this existence, so that we can depend on Him to keep us safe. If we do not admit that this world is a very dangerous place and believe that Jesus Christ will sustain us, His protection for us is limited. Jesus Christ is not a respecter of persons, but, to be under His full protection in this spiritual penal colony, we are required to admit the truth about our condition. To have His protection, or to not have it, has nothing to do with whether or not He loves us.

Our knowledge of, and willingness to face our true condition, gives us the opportunity to praise the Lord and to thank Him for His protection. Our prayers go up to heaven, to the higher realms, like the odors of burning incense, and our thanks and praise draw His protection towards us.

Gen 8:21

> [21]*AND THE LORD SMELLED A SWEET SAVOUR*; AND THE LORD SAID IN HIS HEART, I WILL NOT AGAIN CURSE THE GROUND ANY MORE FOR MAN'S SAKE; FOR THE IMAGINATION OF MAN'S HEART IS EVIL FROM HIS YOUTH; NEITHER WILL I AGAIN SMITE ANY MORE EVERY THING LIVING, AS I HAVE DONE. **KJV**

The carnal Christian would say, *Jehovah just loves the shedding of blood.* The Lord smelling incense is a parable. The Scripture means, *their prayers went up to heaven.*

Jehovah in the Old Testament represents the three Sefirot of the Godhead to us. He is the center point of the seven lower Sefirot, and He is appearing to us today as the Lord Jesus Christ.

The Scripture says, *He smelled the sacrifice,* or the incense, but it means that the person's prayers ascended all the way up to Jehovah, and He became aware of them. Our prayers move the heavens. We pray, and Jehovah, the God of the world above responds, but the ultimate goal is to bring heaven down to earth through the only Mediator between God and man, the man. Christ Jesus.

Kabbalah has the same message as the carnal Church Of course, it differs from the rapture, which is false doctrine, but it is right in line with the Doctrine of Christ, only with more detail.

According to Kabbalah the middle line (column) of Adam Kadmon signifies *Jacob*. Why does Kabbalah assign names to the columns? The purpose of Kabbalah is to find the esoteric, or hidden mysteries of God. Like the Scripture, which can be understood on many levels, the mysteries unfold when we look at the Hebrew text, which is printed without any vowels.

The Hebrew people, the Jews who study or worship in Hebrew, add the vowels as they read the printed letters, and the meaning of the words change, in according with the choice of vowels. When the Scripture was originally written, the Hebrew letters were not even broken down into words. The text of a whole book was one long string of words, just one letter after another.

The Hebrew mind had to decide which letters would end a word and which vowels to impute to each letter. This tells me that the Hebrew language was intended to be read under the anointing. I think that if you gave me a series of English letters without any vowels, it would blow my mind to try to figure out what the words meant.

I have known this for years about the Hebrew language, but now I see that the Scripture is founded on the same principle. How could this be? Kabbalah teaches that the Name, **Jehovah**, appears in three or four Sefirot, Elohim appears in the Names of a couple of Sefirot, and there are different manifestations of the attributes depending upon different circumstances. For example, *Chochmah*-wisdom can be manifesting in *Yesod*, or *Gevurah-force* can be manifesting through *Netzach-overcoming*. It can drive you crazy! There is an upper wisdom and a lower wisdom. How do I know which is which?

Reading the Scripture with spiritual understanding requires us to do the same thing that readers of the Hebrew language do. We have to know where a word begins and ends, and which vowels to use with each word. The only way you can do this, is by reading the Scripture under the anointing, which the Spirit of Revelation of Jesus Christ. I do not see how it is possible any other way, unless you have a spirit of witchcraft, which would give you a false understanding anyway. Without a spiritual anointing guiding you, it is impossible to perceive the secret meaning of the Scripture.

The Church today is in a dire condition of spiritual death when they believe that they cannot change one English word of the King James translation without being cursed. The Scripture is intended to be fluid in accordance with the intention of the anointing. It is not intended to be solid and immovable. It is possible that several people looking at the same Scripture would understand it differently, but I believe that if everyone was truly in Christ, there would be no contradiction.

There are occasions when I do find a contradiction in the Scripture. I found in the Book of Genesis in the account of Jacob wrestling with the angel. I taught for years that the angel who wrestled with Jacob was Christ in Jacob, and that Christ touched Jacob's left thigh (his reproductive part). The left thigh, or left side, typifies harsh spiritual power, meaning that Christ Jesus arose within Jacob and broke Satan's power, which was manifesting in Jacob as fear of his brother, Esau.

But Rabbi Gikatilla, does not see it that way. He believes Jacob was wrestling with an *evil angel*. So, I said, *Lord, am I wrong? I need to know if I am wrong. I have it so very, very strong that it was Christ rising in Jacob and breaking his carnal mind.*

You may recall that Jacob was afraid that he, his whole family, servants and everyone traveling with him, were going to be destroyed by his brother Esau. He prayed and prayed, asking the God of his fathers for help, and suddenly an angel appeared and wrestled with him. There was a conflict between Jacob's carnal mind and Christ Jesus within Jacob. Christ Jesus defeated

Jacob's carnal mind by touching the reproductive part of his carnal mind, which is the *Fiery Serpent*, the one who has the ability to join with Leviathan and bring forth spiritual power in Satan.

Gen 32:24-25

> [24]AND JACOB WAS LEFT ALONE; AND THERE WRESTLED A MAN WITH HIM UNTIL THE BREAKING OF THE DAY.
>
> [25]AND WHEN HE SAW THAT HE PREVAILED NOT AGAINST HIM, HE TOUCHED THE HOLLOW OF HIS THIGH; AND THE HOLLOW OF JACOB'S THIGH WAS OUT OF JOINT, AS HE WRESTLED WITH HIM. **KJV**

Christ Jesus touched the Fiery Serpent and made her impotent to join with Leviathan, and from that day forward, Jacob limped. Satan lost her power over Jacob to make him afraid, and. Christ Jesus became his strength.

We are limited in our ability to manifest Christ Jesus while our carnal mind is in competition with Him. If we are manifesting pride, rebellion or envy, Christ Jesus is limited to what He can do in us and through us, for us or for other people. This is the war I have been talking about in this message.

If you have spiritual power and loving kindness towards other people, and you are judging your own carnal mind, at some point you will ascend into miracle working power. That is what the Scripture teaches. That is what happened to Jacob. He was terrified of his brother Esau, who was a spiritually powerful man, the son of Isaac (who represents harsh judgment). Esau's soul was on the left side, which made him spiritually cruel. He was not serving the living God, and Jacob was terrified.

Jacob prayed all night. Do you think He prayed all night and an angel came down and defeated him? No. When I read the account, that the morning came and Jacob met Esau and they were friends, for the longest time I thought, *Look at that! Jacob had nothing to worry about after all. His brother did not mean him any harm.*

Gen 33:1-4

¹AND JACOB LIFTED UP HIS EYES, AND LOOKED, AND, BEHOLD, ESAU CAME, AND WITH HIM FOUR HUNDRED MEN. AND HE DIVIDED THE CHILDREN UNTO LEAH, AND UNTO RACHEL, AND UNTO THE TWO HANDMAIDS.

²AND HE PUT THE HANDMAIDS AND THEIR CHILDREN FOREMOST, AND LEAH AND HER CHILDREN AFTER, AND RACHEL AND JOSEPH HINDERMOST.

³AND HE PASSED OVER BEFORE THEM, AND BOWED HIMSELF TO THE GROUND SEVEN TIMES, UNTIL HE CAME NEAR TO HIS BROTHER.

⁴*AND ESAU RAN TO MEET HIM, AND EMBRACED HIM, AND FELL ON HIS NECK, AND KISSED HIM: AND THEY WEPT.* **KJV**

The truth is that Esau intended to destroy Jacob and his whole party, but Jacob had a spiritual experience with Christ Jesus (Adam Kadmon in the Old Testament) who was within him. The Angel of the Lord arose in Jacob and defeated Jacob's carnal mind, which was terrified. The Angel of the Lord is never afraid. He rose up and defeated Jacob's carnal mind by touching the Fiery Serpent, the reproductive part of Jacob's left side, so that she could never join with Leviathan again.

Gen 32:31-32

³¹AND AS HE PASSED OVER PENUEL THE SUN ROSE UPON HIM, AND HE HALTED UPON HIS THIGH.

32THEREFORE THE CHILDREN OF ISRAEL EAT NOT OF THE SINEW WHICH SHRANK, WHICH IS UPON THE HOLLOW OF THE THIGH, UNTO THIS DAY: BECAUSE HE TOUCHED THE HOLLOW OF JACOB'S THIGH IN *THE SINEW THAT SHRANK.* **KJV**

The sinew which shrank was Jacob's strength in his carnal mind. The angel of the Lord compensated for the side which was crippled, and the battle was won in the Spirit before the two men ever faced each other in the morning. As soon as Christ Jesus prevailed over Jacob's carnal mind, Esau was defeated and made harmless in the Spirit.

Battling The Carnal Mind

Every battle is within ourselves. We are undefeatable in any and every situation if Christ Jesus has defeated our carnal mind in that situation. If we are manifesting pride or self-preservation in any form, our carnal mind is prevailing and we can lose. You do not win a battle because you answered an altar call or speak in tongues.

You have the victory when Christ Jesus rises to the surface and covers over your carnal mind, because your carnal mind stops you from connecting to the Lord Jesus Christ above. If you are Jewish and reading this message, I would say that your carnal mind is preventing you from contacting *understanding*, the Sefirah who channels *wisdom* and *Keter*.

You, who are down here in the earth, can lose all your power if your carnal mind breaks the marital union between you and the male organ of the middle line. When Satan wants to defeat you, she will seek to find your weakness, to cause you to be angry, for example, or she will tempt you to sin in some way. She does this for the specific purpose of breaking the marital union between Christ in you and the male organ of the glorified Jesus Christ, so you are cut off from the spiritual power you need for the battle. Your biggest battle is with your own carnal mind.

Satan will try to make you angry, envious or disobedient, anything to cut you off from that power. The day you get this revelation, that you receive your sight, that you look into the motives of your own heart and say, *I am not going to yield to these thoughts or these emotions because I have an assignment in Christ Jesus,* you are undefeatable. You have to get on top of your carnal mind. We have the glorified Jesus Christ in this dispensation, so it is much easier for us than it was for the men of Israel.

We have to get past saying *it is impossible. I am afraid. I am too old. I am too sick.* If the Lord is truly calling you, if it is not your pride, nothing is impossible for you. He will equip you to do whatever He is calling you to do. The power is in the glorified Jesus Christ. Satan is down here in the earth cutting us off from that power by causing us to sin. Our biggest battle is with the hidden sins of our own heart.

We need to learn to recognize the thought patterns of the carnal mind. It is possible to have *good* thoughts out of the carnal mind, so the battle is distinguishing between the good thoughts of the carnal mind and the thoughts of Christ. What we think is a good idea may arise out of an *evil motive*.

Many people have been serving God for decades, but their spirit has not been purified. Recognizing the evil and crushing it by the power of Christ purifies us. The Scripture says, *He who has this hope in him purifies himself.* He who has the hope of bringing the unlimited power of the Godhead down into their earth, is the man who purifies himself.

1 Jn 3:3

[3]AND EVERY MAN THAT *HATH THIS HOPE IN HIM PURIFIETH HIMSELF*, EVEN AS HE IS PURE. **KJV**

The gifts and the calling of God are without repentance in the Holy Spirit, but eternal life is in Christ Jesus, who requires us to repent. If you are hoping for eternal life and you are not purifying yourself, you are deceived.

Rom 11:29

[29]FOR THE GIFTS AND CALLING OF GOD ARE WITHOUT REPENTANCE. **KJV**

DIAGRAMS

Introducing Adam Kadmon
Diagram #1
by Cecilia H. Bryant

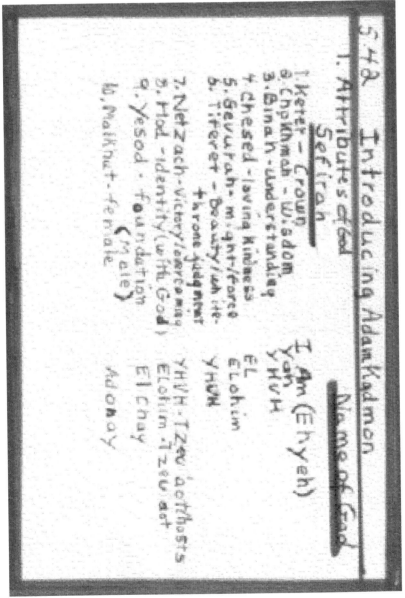

Introducing Adam Kadmon
Diagram #2
by Cecilia H. Bryant

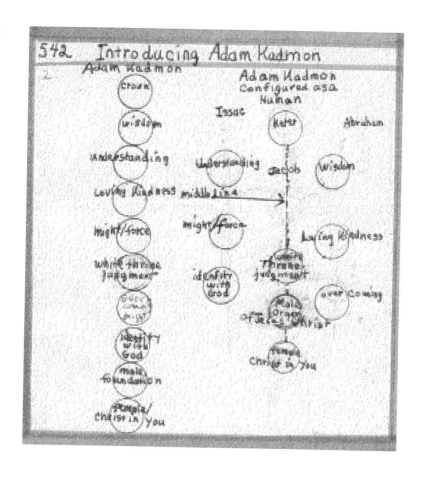

TABLE OF REFERENCES

THE LOCK & THE KEY

Sexual Mores In The Last Days

Sheila R. Vitale
Christ-Centered Kabbalah

ABOUT THE AUTHOR

SHEILA R. VITALE

Sheila R. Vitale is the Spiritual Leader, Founding Teacher and Pastor of _Christ-Centered Kabbalah (CCK)_. Pastor Vitale has been expounding upon the Torah (Scripture) through a unique Judeo-Christian lens for nearly three decades, and has an international following. As head of the teaching ministries, she disseminates Judeo-Christian literature, both printed and online, to individuals around the world.

In addition to managing CCK, Pastor Vitale is an illustrator of spiritual principles, researcher, translator, social commentator, lecturer, movie, TV and theater critic, and author. She has given more than 1,000 _LEM_ lectures that explain hundreds of spiritual principles, all of which may be purchased on CDs or as downloadable MP3s. In addition, beginning in the year 2013, Videos of Pastor Vitale's lectures became available for purchase on DVDs or downloadable MP4s. She has written more than 21 books based upon the Old and New Testaments and authentic Rabbinic Kabbalah, including _The Noah Chronicles, The Crime of the Calf_ and _The Three Israels_, as well as unique and esoteric translations of canonical Biblical texts such as _The Prophesies of Daniel, Chapter 8_, _The Prophesies of Daniel According to Kabbalah, Chapter 11_, _The Crime of the Calf_, _Sophia_ and _The Common Salvation_. Some of her forthcoming publications include _1 Corinthians, Chapter 11_.

KABBALAH AND
CHRIST-CENTERED KABBALAH

Sheila Vitale has been studying Torah (Scripture) and the New Testament, in-depth, since the 1970s, and began to teach her understanding of it, which she calls The Doctrine of Christ, in January of 1988. In the year 2000, she began to study and teach the Jewish spiritual philosophy of authentic *Lurian Kabbalah.* Since then, she has woven her continuously evolving understanding of *The Doctrine of Christ* and *Lurian Kabbalah* into a fascinating and unparalleled course of study that she calls, *Christ-Centered Kabbalah. Christ-Centered Kabbalah* is based upon her original research in the Hebrew text of the Torah, the foundational books of *Philosophical Kabbalah,* such as *The Zohar,* and the Greek text of *The New Testament.* She was teaching *The Doctrine of Christ* with *Lurian Kabbalah* for at least one year when, in 2001, the Lord Jesus Christ divided the ministries and established Christ-*Centered Kabbalah.*

She has also been studying the authentic Jewish Kabbalah of several Rabbinic scholars, including *Moses Nachmanides* (Ramban), *Moses Cordovero (*Ramak*)* and *Isaac Luria (*The Ari*)* since the year 2000. She has read many of the English translations of their writings, including *Ramban's The Gate of Reward, Ramak's Pardes Rimonim (Orchard of Pomegranates*), and *The* teachings *of the Ari,* as written by his student, *Chayyim Vital,* in *The Tree of Life: The Palace of Adam Kadmon,* and *The Gate of Reincarnations.*

Sheila Vitale received the call to study *kosher* Jewish Kabbalah in August of the year 2000 while evangelizing in Greenville, South Carolina. At that time, the Spirit of God directed her to read and study the teachings of Rabbi Luria, as written by his student, *Chayyim Vital,* in *The Tree of Life: The Palace of Adam Kadmon.* She could not understand it, but continued to read anyway. Shortly thereafter, she saw an angel enter into her, and the eyes of her understanding began to open. Pastor Vitale attributes her ability to understand and teach authentic Jewish Kabbalah and *Christ-Centered Kabbalah,* which she believes is beyond the grasp of the human mind, to the Lord Jesus Christ.

She often cautions her students about the dangers of Qabalah that is not kosher. She asks everyone who would like to know more about her to please note that all Kabbalah is not kosher (authentic). Pastor Vitale teaches *authentic Kabbalah, which glorifies God*, and she shuns the *occult Qabalah* of personal power, which, all too frequently, is used to control unsuspecting persons, acquire wealth by spiritual power, or punish one's enemies.

She continues today to manage *Christ-Centered Kabbalah* and to write and teach about *authentic Kabbalah and Christ-Centered Kabbalah*.

BEGINNINGS, INSPIRATION AND CALLING

Sheila Vitale was born into a Jewish family, and began her spiritual journey as a child when her mother enrolled her as a student in an Orthodox Hebrew school. She also attended synagogue on Shabbat during that time, where she experienced the Spirit of God for the first time. Such a deep longing for God was stirred up in her that she wept. She was touched so profoundly that she became desperate to attend yeshiva (Jewish high school) but her parents could not afford to send her.

She became very ill around the age of 11, and has battled with chronic illness ever since. (Her most recent struggle against premature death came in 1990, when she spent three months in the hospital.) Her illnesses led her to cry out to God, seeking a deeper understanding of what was happening to her.

Much later, as an adult, after years of searching, she, once again, experienced the Spirit that had brought her to tears, but this time it was in *Gospel Revivals Ministries*, a Pentecostal church where Deliverance Ministry was emphasized. She had desired a deeper understanding of Scripture since her early years, so she began to attend church regularly. She read at least one

Chapter of the Bible every day, but did not understand what she was reading. Scripture was difficult for her, and she struggled with the task. After about six months, however, while reading the Bible, she saw a vision of the angel with the little book described in Chapter 10 of the Book of Revelation, Verse 8. She began to understand the Bible after that, but several more years had to pass before she began to receive Revelation knowledge of the Scripture.

Sheila Vitale studied the Bible and Deliverance Ministry for about seven years under the teaching of *Charles Holzhauser*, the Pastor of *Gospel Revivals Ministries*, in Mount Sinai, NY. Sometimes she attended as many as five teaching services each week, as well as studying for endless hours to gain key insight into her faith. She also edited *Pastor Holzhauser's* books during that time. After that, she studied independently under the influence and direction of the Holy Spirit, before founding *Living Epistles Ministries (LEM)*.

She began to learn authentic *Lurian Kabbalah* in October of 2000 and to teach it in 2001. After that, in November of 2002, she began to teach Kabbalah creatively. Thus, after serving 12 years with *LEM*, she undertook a second mission and founded *Christ-Centered Kabbalah*, which emerged as a vehicle for the publishing and distribution of her unique brand of Kabbalah.

WRITINGS AND WORK TODAY

Sheila Vitale's signature work is the three volumes of *The Alternate Translation Bible*: *The Alternate Translation Of The Old Testament*, *The Alternate Translation of the New Testament* and *The Alternate Translation of the Book of Revelation*. *The Alternate Translation Bible* is an esoteric translation of the Scripture, and is not intended to replace traditional translations. *The Book of Revelation* and several other books that Pastor Vitale has written have been translated into Spanish.

She is currently submitting *CCK* books for retail sale through *Barnes & Noble*. Paperback and digital versions of the books are also available at Amazon.com and the official *CCK* website. She also has an *Author's* website which displays all of her books, as well as several photographs of her and a short bio. She also writes for the *Blog* on the CCK website, where a detailed review of radio talk show host, Alex Jones', interview of Louis Farrakhan is posted. She has also delivered hundreds of messages, many of which have been transcribed and may be viewed free of charge on the *Christ-Centered Kabbalah* website.

She also continues to publish and make a wide range of Biblical translations and educational materials available for free on the *CCK* official website, as well as providing free video lectures to the public through *the Christ-Centered Kabbalah YouTube channel.* She also has another YouTube channel called *Short Clip by Sheila R. Vitale,* where she posts short, focused messages which average 15 minutes each.

PASTOR VITALE TODAY

Sheila Vitale serves a range of ecclesiastical, educational, and administrative functions from her headquarters in Port Jefferson Station, New York. Operating in the Offices of Evangelist, Prophet, Teacher of Apostolic Doctrine and Pastor, she continues delivering her powerful messages on a range of topics, from movie reviews and social commentaries to esoteric interpretations of the Scripture, Torah, Messiah, Noah, Judgment, Science, Ascension, Immortality and Reincarnation and Pagan & Judeo-Christian Spiritual Roots.

She has dedicated her life to studying and teaching Judeo-Christian spiritual principles, and continues to focus daily on studying, teaching and writing. In February of 2016, she joined other *CCK* teachers to dedicate a new *CCK* Building in Gray Court, South Carolina.

She is also a philanthropic individual who supports numerous charitable organizations, including *Feed the Children, Judicial Watch, World Vision, Lighthouse Mission,* and *The International Fellowship of Christians and Jews.* She also helps local groups such as the *Terryville Fire Department.* In her spare time, Pastor Vitale enjoys watching movies, attending plays and partaking of cuisines from different cultures. An avid traveler, she has visited numerous countries in Europe and Africa as well as many cities in the United States.

Christ-Centered Kabbalah
Sheila R Vitale,
Pastor, Teacher & Founder
~ The Compleat Kabbalah ~
PO Box 562, Port Jefferson Station, New York 11776, USA
Christ-CenteredKabbalah.org *or* Books@Christ-CenteredKabbalah.org
(631) 331-1493

56936038R00033

Made in the USA
San Bernardino, CA
15 November 2017